Field Notes from Y

Apprentice to Plac

Teresa Jordan
with a Foreword by Gretel Ehrlich

Johnson Books • BOULDER

Published by Johnson Books, a division of Johnson Publishing Company, 1880 South 57th Court, Boulder, Colorado 80301. E-mail: books@jpcolorado.com.

9 8 7 6 5 4 3 2 1

Cover design by Debra Topping.
All artwork is from the sketchbooks of Teresa Jordan except "Evening Moon" by Chiura Obata, used by permission.

Library of Congress Cataloging-in-Publication Data
Jordan, Teresa.
    Field notes from Yosemite: apprentice to place / Teresa Jordan.
        p. cm.
Includes bibliographical references.
    ISBN 1-55566-274-9
    1. Yosemite National Park (Calif.)—Pictorial works. 2. Yosemite
National Park (Calif.)—Description and travel. 3. Natural
history—California—Yosemite National Park. 4. Watercolor
painting—California—Yosemite National Park. 5. Jordan, Teresa. I.
Title.
    F868.Y6 J65 2002
    979.4'47'00222—dc21   2002015771

Printed in the United States by
Johnson Printing
1880 South 57th Court
Boulder, Colorado 80301

DATE DUE

GAYLORD		PRINTED IN U.S.A.

odge for nearly two decades,

are their love of Yosemite

music and art

Contents

Foreword

Gretel Ehrlich

Ranch-raised, Yale-educated, resident of hay meadows, mountains, and cities, Teresa Jordan has made her way to America's first and most treasured national park and made it her own. *Field Notes from Yosemite* is her apprenticeship in watercolors and text to rock, tree, and glacier—her small homage to that singular place.

John Muir, father of the park and founder of the Sierra Club, wrote this about an autumn day on the valley floor: "I spring to my feet crying: 'Heaven and earth! Rock is not light, not heavy, not transparent, not opaque, but every pore gushes, glows like a thought with immortal life!'" Such is the homage Jordan pays to this place, guided by Muir as well as the lovely paintings of Chiura Obata. As Jordan swings between her city life and her pilgrimages to Yosemite's mountain fastness, we swing with her and are reminded that apprenticeship, not expertise, is what allows us to see, and to revel in, the glories of the Range of Light.

Prologue

Apprentice
to Place

Dorothee said, "Happiness is such a *distinct* state." We were halfway up Mount Hoffman, taking a rest with our backs against the craggy trunks of Sierra junipers. With our friend Diana, we had set up base camp at May Lake the night before, and now the three of us were basking in the simple grace of being healthy and strong and together under the generous September sun in the High Sierra. As we gazed across an alpine meadow toward Half Dome in the distance, I thought: happiness *is* a state apart, something that seems to tingle through every cell in the body. We felt alive, present, completely at home.

But of course we were not at home. In fact, we had gone to great lengths to leave home in order to gather here, Diana coming from Montana, Dorothee and I from Utah. Like millions of others each year, we had come to a national park to relax, unwind, and reconnect with nature, which was to say with a simpler side of ourselves. Following in a tradition that could be traced back through Americans such as John Muir and Henry David Thoreau but had roots in the Bible and other sacred texts, we had turned to the wild for regeneration.

Like almost everyone I know, I juggle a myriad of responsibilities and deadlines and often find myself in a state of near panic. Almost every day, I run into one friend or another who answers the query, "How are you?" with a litany of overwork, straining to pick her way through what the writer Kim Stafford called a "pomegranate of impossible tasks."

To try to renew a sense of balance, an increasing number of us escape to the national parks. While our population has not quite doubled in the past fifty years, our use of national parks has increased by over eight and a half times. For the past several years, annual visitation has edged toward the three hundred million mark, "as if," in the words of the *New York Times*, "every man, woman and child in the country visited at least one park a year."

Behind this mass exodus from daily life is a desire to mark out a few days when we can put our lives on hold and seek something more primal, when our choices are fewer and the fax and the e-mail and the cell phone don't sound their little alarms. We may have had our heads down, blindly following something—even work we love—but here in the wild we throw back our shoulders, take a big breath, and look out to the far horizon. We challenge ourselves physically and find that we have not turned entirely to mush. We reconnect with the natural world and feel a childlike delight in the beauty of even its smallest details: the suede of green moss at the base of a tree, the ancient twist and sheen of roots, the smooth comfort of a river-polished stone that fits perfectly in the cup of a

hand. We breathe in the clear brace of early morning, shriek at the icy shock of a mountain pond, melt into the warmth of a boulder in the afternoon sun. And then we go back to our "normal" lives, and the stress starts all over again.

Life hasn't always been split in this way. Only during the twentieth century did the majority of the world's population find itself working in buildings rather than outside. And now our new century is the first in the history of civilization to begin with more people living in cities than in the country.

I grew up on a Wyoming ranch and spent my youth outside whenever I wasn't in school. Nature and work were intimately intertwined. Now, like the vast majority of Americans, I work in a metropolitan area and venture many miles from home when I want to enjoy significant time out-of-doors.

"We were born of wilderness and we respond to it more than we sometimes realize," wrote Wallace Stegner in 1990. "We depend upon wilderness increasingly for relief from the termite life we have created." Stegner stressed this need as a reason to preserve our wild places; ironically, in our search for balance, we have flocked to national parks and wilderness areas in such hordes that we trample them under the weight of our numbers.

"I love this place," wrote Yosemite Park Ranger David Siegenthaler in 2000 as part of a display that emphasized the efforts being undertaken to balance the health of Yosemite's natural resources with the ever-increasing number of visitors:

But what distinguishes love from self-indulgence? I presume this means that there are many people like me who love to be here and experience Yosemite on their own terms—and that those "many" in our simple personal pursuits are collectively damaging the very things we profess to love. ...

So what is love to do? How does one love Yosemite in the company of so many other lovers?

I first visited Yosemite briefly in the spring of 1999. I couldn't wait to get back and returned for a glorious three weeks the next fall. In 2001 I came back yet again for ten days in August. With each visit I felt more attached and at home than the time before, but also more haunted by the quandary that Ranger Siegenthaler so eloquently pondered. If we love a place, we want to protect it. But what can a single visitor do except not visit at all?

Out of this question came others. What might happen if I started to think of Yosemite not as a place to escape to as often as possible but as a place that could teach me ways of living that would make escape less necessary? For those of us who need the wild for balance, isn't there a way to incorporate the wild, or incorporate the balance we find in the wild, into our daily lives, if only for a moment each day? What might happen to our cities if we began to look at them with the same sensitivity to natural processes that comes so easily to us in Yosemite? I began to think of myself not as a visitor to this place so much as an apprentice to it, seeking out lessons that would sustain me at home.

But how could I apprentice myself to Yosemite in the too-brief spans of occasional visits? National parks earn their designations because they are extraordinary places. Because they are extraordinary places, they inspire extensive study and comment, and a wealth of accessible knowledge accumulates around them. I decided to look at what others had learned about this one place, with the hope that I would better understand how to learn about others.

I turned first to what drew me to Yosemite in the first place, the trees and the rocks. Perhaps if I learned more about them in Yosemite, I could look at the foliage and geology that surrounded my urban home with new appreciation. I brought a host of guidebooks to the task as well as my paint box and set out each day for long hikes, quiet hours painting, and the delight of trying to identify and learn a few new things.

I turned as well to the examples of others who had apprenticed themselves to this place, especially John Muir, Yosemite's sterling apprentice and the first man to understand its geology in depth, and Chiura Obata, a Japanese-born painter whose work I discovered on my first visit to the park. The six weeks he spent in the High Sierra in 1927 kept him coming back for the rest of his life. Being in the world and painting it were

almost indistinguishable for Obata, and as my own love of painting deepened, I saw in him a powerful model. I was also drawn to him because he so successfully carried his love of wild places with him wherever he went. Yosemite sustained him even during the years of World War II, when he was imprisoned at California's Tanforan Racetrack and at Topaz, a dusty relocation camp in the Utah desert.

I took lessons, too, from others, past and present, including that exemplary scholar of trees, Donald Culross Peattie, and a rich array of park rangers, geologists, naturalists, writers, and others who love this place with a passion that translates into knowledge. Out of all their teachings, these musings were born.

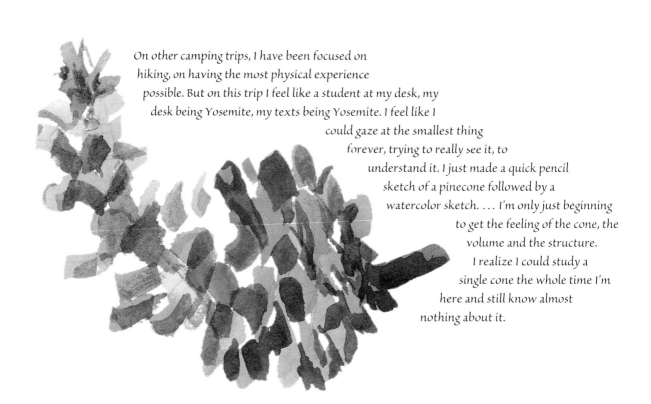

On other camping trips, I have been focused on
hiking, on having the most physical experience
possible. But on this trip I feel like a student at my desk, my
desk being Yosemite, my texts being Yosemite. I feel like I
could gaze at the smallest thing
forever, trying to really see it, to
understand it. I just made a quick pencil
sketch of a pinecone followed by a
watercolor sketch. … I'm only just beginning
to get the feeling of the cone, the
volume and the structure.
I realize I could study a
single cone the whole time I'm
here and still know almost
nothing about it.

I painted a tree up Mount
Hoffman a few days ago, and I
like the strength and thrust of
the trunk, but the foliage is
generic. As I look at it now, I
can't even tell what sort of
tree it is.

Tonight I've been looking at
Obata's trees, and I can almost
always tell what species they are.
This makes me realize that there
are two types of simplicity,
one that comes from quick
generality and another, more
satisfying type that comes from
real understanding, where
everything but the truest essence
can fall away.

When Hal and I spent twelve days on the Colorado River a few years ago, I wrote in my journal, "How can we keep this sense of reverence in our daily lives?" Life, as they say, intruded, and here I am again, tramping up a mountain, trying to regain a sense of peace.

Apprentice to Trees

By the end of my second trip to Yosemite, I was growing cocky about my increasing knowledge of the area's trees. But one morning I looked up at the towering specimen that dominated the front entrance to the Cedar Lodge in El Portal and found myself befuddled. It wasn't a pine because the needles weren't in clusters; it wasn't a fir because its needles were round; it certainly didn't have the lacy foliage of incense-cedar. The short, dense foliage was reminiscent of larch, but the tree was blue-green rather than dark- or yellow-green, and larches don't grow in this area.

I went inside and asked the woman at the front desk, who in turn consulted someone in the back. Neither of them could identify the tree, so I took a small branch with me and asked several rangers until one identified my tree as *Cedrus deodara,* or deodar cedar, a favorite of landscapers. It came originally from the Himalayas and was a true cedar, he explained. There are no true cedars native to this continent; Yosemite's incense-cedars are more similar to the arborvitaes.

What does it matter if we know the names of the trees? Why should we care if a motel names itself after an imported tree rather than a native, or if we even know the difference between a fir and a pine? It mattered a great deal to our ancestors, for the forests were their pharmacies and grocery stores. Now most of us "need" to know more about lumber than we do about the trees from which it was cut. What to choose for the deck? What to use for shelves?

We humans have a great capacity for discernment; our very survival depends on how well we hunt and gather, and we learn to pick and choose among what serves our needs and what is superfluous or even dangerous. But today we use that ability largely for product recognition. A broad swath of American teens can unerringly discern between a garment bought at the Gap and one that comes from Old Navy, though these differences escape the rest of us. But how many know the difference between a sugar pine and a ponderosa? And why should they care?

"Until one knows the name of a tree one cannot ask questions about it, or trace it in books of reference, or, indeed, even think of it clearly," wrote Donald Culross Peattie in his charming and informative classic, *A Natural History of Western Trees*. He went on to suggest that any place we have enjoyed will mean more to us if we recognize its trees, for their particularity will serve "to keep more truly alive the memories of that happiness."

Missing the fact that the big tree outside the Cedar Lodge came originally from India rather than from the High Sierra was much as if I had wandered through an Alaskan park with a group of Tlingit totem poles in one section and a Chinese pagoda in another. If I had never seen a pagoda before and interpreted it as a different sort of totem rather than a memorial to Chinese immigrants, I would be blind to part of the record of that place, deaf to a side of its story. The fact that neither the employees of the Cedar Lodge nor I even recognized the tree as a cedar meant that we missed the fact that the place was named not for an abstraction—there are cedars in them thar hills—or even for the native incense-cedars on the grounds but for the specific tree that towered over the front entrance.

Sooner or later, almost every naturalist uses the metaphor of nature as a book that one can learn to read. John Muir liked the trope of the palimpsest, the parchment or tablet where each succeeding chapter is written on top of the one that preceded it. Why learn to read this text? Peattie suggests for the simple joy of it, but what, exactly, does that mean?

I'd always meant to learn the names of the trees. I knew many of those that grew around my home, at least in general terms: cottonwood, willow, red osier dogwood, box elder. I didn't really know the difference between a coyote willow and a white willow, and when we lived in Nevada it took me some time to notice that the big cottonwood next to our barn had noticeably different leaves than the cottonwoods I had grown up with in Wyoming (black cottonwood, *Populus trichocarpa,* in Nevada; plains cottonwood, *Populus deltoides,* in Wyoming). The names of the trees were something that I, like a lot of people, intended to get around to one of these days.

On my second trip to Yosemite, I decided to get serious. I armed myself with references—Peterson's *Field Guide to Western Trees*, Stephen Arno's *Discovering Sierra Trees*, and Peattie's *A Natural History of Western Trees.*

But where to begin? The good thing about looking at the trees of a particular place is that region alone simplifies your task, and I decided in the beginning to further limit myself to conifers. Arno listed nineteen of them in *Discovering Sierra Trees*; I figured if I learned half of them during this visit, I'd have made a good start.

I began with the big divisions. What *is* the difference between a fir and a pine? The needles on pine trees are round and come in clusters bound by a papery envelope (a "sheaf") at their base (single-leaf piñon has only a single needle but still has the papery sheaf). Their cones hang down. Firs have single needles that are flat or four-sided. Their cones stick up. What's hard about this? Incense-cedars, with their scaly foliage and ropy bark, are easy to identify, as are the giant sequoia, at least in maturity, when they tower over everything else and their heavy bark glows red in the sun. I was getting good.

But then I found myself at the base of a towering tree with thick gray bark. Its lowest branches were yards beyond my reach, but I picked up a fallen twig. Single needles. A fir. Then I looked up and saw cones hanging down. A pine. I turned to the back of Peattie and began to wind my way through the couplets that make up a botanical key. Leaves or no leaves? Leaves. Very large leaves or not so large? Not so large. Leaves needle- or scale-like or not needle- or scale-like? Needle-like. And so on until, after learning some new vocabulary from the glossary (the "margin" of a needle? A "stalked" leaf?), I ended up at Douglas fir. When I read the tree's description, I realized I had followed the key correctly, and I felt as excited as a kid with a decoder ring. And I realized, too, that I wasn't the first one the Doug fir had thrown for a loop. Beginning in the 1800s, the tree had been variously classified as a pine, a fir, a spruce, a yew, and a hemlock before its quirks earned it a designation of its own, *pseudotsuga*, or false hemlock. I like a tree that breaks the rules.

With its two stout needles, lodgepole is also known as the roach clip tree.

Little by little, a world of clues began to reveal itself. One day I stopped on Highway 41 on my way to Wawona and looked out over the A-Rock/Steamboat burn, determined to read the trees by their blackened skeletons. In time I learned to recognize the ponderosas by the optimistic upturn of their branches and the sugar pines by the lumbering way they thrust their arms out and down, like little kids pretending to be monsters. I lay down on the soft forest floor of the Mariposa Grove and realized, as I looked up at the trees stretching to the sky, that I could tell sugar pines and white firs apart even from a great distance by the silhouettes of their foliage: clumpy on the sugar pine, ferny on the fir—"fir-ny," a little mnemonic gift. As I began to meet trees as individuals, learning their names and home grounds, their likes and dislikes, their quirks and affections, I began, as well, to recognize their talents.

Douglas fir,
the bottlebrush tree.

Tree as barometer: the split-trunk bull pine with its frothy foliage that lives so happily in the mild climate around El Portal seems just as satisfied on the banks of Hetch Hetchy reservoir, two thousand feet higher. Since snow weighs the bull pine down and breaks it apart, the tree's presence tells us that Hetch Hetchy is unusually mild for its elevation.

Tree as sociologist: after a day spent wandering the Mariposa Grove, I saw a Douglas-fir cone along a path to the parking lot. I hadn't seen a Doug fir all day, so I asked a ranger. "There are only two of them that I know of in the whole grove," he told me, "way up at the top." Someone must have picked up the cone as a souvenir—a violation of park policy—but laid it guiltily to rest before heading home.

Something in us aspires to the life of trees; we hear it in our turns of phrase. A young girl is "willowy"; an ironworker "strong as an oak." Some trees are so grand that we pale in comparison. "You draw yourself up achingly," wrote Peattie of walking among the redwoods, "trying to find some undiscovered worth in yourself to add a cubit to mere manhood." When John Muir introduced Ralph Waldo Emerson to the sequoias in Mariposa Grove,

The Doug-fir cone is characterized by its little three-toed bracts. Legend has it that, once upon a time, the Doug fir became annoyed at the mice nibbling away at its seeds. When they wouldn't leave, it clamped its cones tight, trapping them all inside.

Emerson said with quiet awe, "There were giants in those days."

I suspect it's the deepening of these relationships that Peattie referred to when he suggested that learning the names of the trees gives us pleasure. We can appreciate the forest, but when individual trees step out from the crowd, something more personal occurs—call it affection. It's the difference between wandering the streets of a foreign land, charmed by the quaint habits of the natives, and having someone introduce herself and invite you home to meet Papa and the kids.

To meet the genus *Sequoia*, for instance, is to be invited among the most aristocratic plants on earth.

The California redwoods that live along the coast are the tallest trees in the world; their sisters, the giant sequoias in Yosemite and other isolated groves in the Sierras, are the most massive. A single mature sequoia can tower thirty stories high and yield 120,000 board feet, theoretically enough to build a subdivision. But no one would attempt such a task, for the wood is brittle. Early loggers couldn't quit felling the giants—they were thrilled by the challenge—but they left most of the massive chunks of shattered timber in place, using mere scraps for toothpicks, grape stakes, and shingles.

The small sequoia cones seem formed from many pairs of lips, whispering of all the things possible if only one of its seeds sprouts and lives its full life of two or three thousand years.

Sequoia cones are no bigger than hen's eggs; their seeds are smaller than flakes of oatmeal and so insubstantial that it takes three thousand of them to make up an ounce. But from such humble beginnings, the trees can live for millennia—the Grizzly Giant in the Mariposa Grove, for instance, was already six hundred years old at the birth of Christ. At that age it was still adolescent, its brown bark just beginning to turn red. It wouldn't be fully mature for another four centuries.

Each adult sequoia is a miracle. During its lifetime, one tree may produce half a billion seeds, but fewer than five hundred of them will ever take root. Of such seedlings, only one in ten thousand will survive to maturity, which means that at the end of their unimaginably long lives, only one in twenty sequoias will leave a direct descendant in this world.

Supporting each giant is a root system that may spread out over a circumference of a hundred and fifty feet. During the growing season, a mature sequoia needs eight hundred to a thousand gallons of water a day. If this quantity is not available within its reach, it will draw on the water source of one of its brothers, for it's a communal creature with subterranean connections.

However effective as a supply system, the roots are shallow. Old sequoias never die, the bumper sticker might read, they just fall over. Yosemite's Grizzly Giant leans at an angle of seventeen degrees; someday its demise will register on the Richter scale. After that it will take another thousand years to return to the earth out of which it came: its bark, two feet thick in places and laced with tannins, is as fire-resistant as asbestos, as inhospitable to bugs and bacteria as steel. In Peattie's words, such a tree is "practically a geological phenomenon."

Such facts are the stuff of Ripley's *Believe It or Not*, but I have only touched the surface. And however much sequoias overshadow more common trees, each species in turn yields up its own fascination, its individual story.

Some time ago, my husband and I visited Ukraine on a cultural exchange. One night in Kiev, greatly fatigued, we became separated from our group. We had a map, but as both it and the street signs were written in the Cyrillic alphabet, we were helpless. We had been lost in Europe and Latin America before, and even though neither of us spoke another language fluently, we could pick up enough clues from a sister tongue to orient ourselves. Now, unable to even sound out the alphabet, we were functionally illiterate.  The signs that could have led us back to our group had no more meaning than filigree.

If nature is a book, it's written in a language many of us can't decipher. But just as learning a few words and phrases of a foreign language can transform a person's experience of travel, entering into the world of trees allows us access to something hidden from us before.

After I returned from Yosemite the last time, my husband and I spent the winter in a condominium overlooking Salt Lake City. Every day I walked past a big pine along the front walk without paying much attention. Then one day I stopped to look at it closely.

Needles in bunches of two; cinnamon-colored, exfoliating bark; small, dense cones. I couldn't find it in my western tree books, but a more knowledgeable friend identified it as Scotch pine. At first I was disappointed. I wanted it to be native, a cousin, perhaps, of one of the trees I had grown to know in Yosemite. But then I realized it was connected to Yosemite after all: like John Muir, it was an immigrant thriving in a newly found home.

The giant sequoias are named for Chief Sequoyah, the Cherokee leader who invented an alphabet and transcribed his language. Written language, he knew, would allow the history and knowledge of his people to thrive beyond the reach of the tribe's individual members. It was a way for them to be connected with the larger world. That's what words do for us: they arc across space and transcend time. Naming lets us recognize the connections among the many parts of our lives.

As I'm learning the names of the trees, the real question is why I never learned them before. ... It seems rude, sort of like teaching a class for a year and never learning the names of the students. Or, more to the point, taking a course from a gifted professor and never being able to recognize her on the street.

Ponderosa Pine

"puzzle bark"

Incense-Cedar

ropy and braided

Sugar Pine

dimensional and reddish
"gouged"

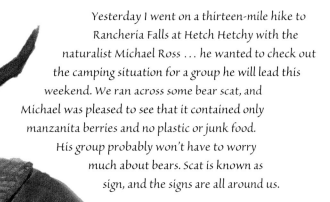

Yesterday I went on a thirteen-mile hike to
Rancheria Falls at Hetch Hetchy with the
naturalist Michael Ross … he wanted to check out
the camping situation for a group he will lead this
weekend. We ran across some bear scat, and
Michael was pleased to see that it contained only
manzanita berries and no plastic or junk food.
His group probably won't have to worry
much about bears. Scat is known as
sign, and the signs are all around us.

Update: Just got a note from
Michael about the camping trip.
His group was visited by one of the
most aggressive bears he had ever
encountered, a mama who
had grown almost entirely
dependent on human
food. At one point she even rushed in and took a bag
from between two campers. Soon after their visit, the
campground was closed in an attempt to discourage her
bad habits. Just goes to remind me that we don't always
find all the signs we need.

*Apprentice
to Rocks*

"You folks just spent twenty bucks to get into a place that is falling apart." The speaker is Ranger Shelton Johnson, and the sweet voice of his clarinet has called us together for a nature walk in Yosemite Meadow. Johnson is part pied piper and part renaissance man: an award-winning poet, he trained as a classical musician before joining the Park Service and today is dressed in the period uniform of a Buffalo Soldier for a talk that he will give later on the Ninth Cavalry Battalion of African American soldiers who guarded Yosemite in 1903. Right now he is speaking about rocks, specifically the granitic rocks that make up Yosemite's domes and monoliths, and pointing to the grand arches that formed as the layers of granite were weakened by cracks and then "exfoliated," or broke away.

Steady as a rock, solid as a rock, hard as a rock—such phrases sound like nonsense in the great arc of Yosemite's creation. Beginning a hundred million years ago and more, in dozens of separate episodes, magma flowed from the fires of middle earth to solidify miles underground under great pressure and then thrust up through the earth's crust, only to wear down under the forces of wind and rain and earthquakes, rivers and glaciers and time. With such a biography, rock seems fluid, plastic. On the vast scale of the earth's history, rock seems downright ephemeral.

The forces that shaped Yosemite in the past are shaping it still as exposed terrain wears down at the same time that upthrust continues. In a million years, Yosemite will be as different from what it is now as it was a million years in the past. As Johnson quips near the end of our time together, "You spent twenty bucks to get into a place that isn't finished yet."

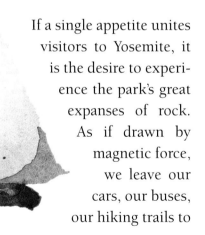

If a single appetite unites visitors to Yosemite, it is the desire to experience the park's great expanses of rock. As if drawn by magnetic force, we leave our cars, our buses, our hiking trails to scramble up the granite or lie prostrate across it. The most athletic cling to the three-thousand-foot face of El Capitan like spiders; the less nimble flatten their palms on the sun-warmed smoothness of boulders at Olmstead Point.

What is it about rock—and specifically about granite—that so comforts us? (I am using the word "granite" in the broadest sense, as a generalization for the variety of granitic rocks that make up Yosemite. Most are heavy with plagioclase, a calcium-rich feldspar, which makes them technically granodiorites.)

Granite is an igneous rock, solidified from liquid magma. There are two types of igneous rock—volcanic, which was liquid when it erupted through the earth's crust and cooled so quickly that, like glass, it experienced little or no crystallization; and plutonic—named for Pluto, god of the underworld—which slowly solidified deep underground, allowing crystals to form, rising to the surface gradually through the aeons as overburden eroded away and shifting tectonic plates thrust it upward. Granite is plutonic, and its crystals give it its grainy texture as well as its name; "grainy" and "granite" derive from the same root.

Yosemite's granite was born in Hades and has ascended nearly to heaven, as anyone who stands atop El Capitan or Half Dome will attest. Perhaps it is this ascension that grips us on an archetypal level. Granite is scoured clean by its trials and ordeals. There is something pure and strong about it, yet fragile, too, as we see its cracks and fissures and, where glaciers or floods haven't taken the evidence away, the talus slopes of its gradual demise. Perhaps it calls out to us with the strength we aspire to even as it reassures us with its own vulnerabilities and scars of experience. Rock is rock and we are human, both shaped by the hand of God: imperfect, impermanent, and beautiful.

Mountains are born, they grow to maturity, they wear down: this simple life cycle, so similar to our own but played out over an incomprehensible span of years, comforts me somehow. I can't walk among Yosemite's granites without musing about time. Years ago, in Jackson Hole, Wyoming, I heard the Chickasaw author Linda Hogan read from *Mean Spirit*, a novel of Native American life. At the end of her presentation, someone from the

audience asked, "Is it true that your people believe in ghosts?" Hogan answered the question with one of her own: "Is it true *your* people believe in time?"

Hogan's wry response amused me, but it also struck the mark. Like almost everyone else I know, I hunger for time. I never have enough; I am literally starved for it. There just isn't *enough* time. I think of D. H. Lawrence's famous short story from the 1920s, "The Rocking Horse Winner," in which a young boy, driven by his parents' insatiable appetite for money, rocks himself into a deathly exhaustion. If Lawrence were to return these many years later, I wonder if he might not choose the lust for time

as the fatal hunger of our age. But what *is* time, anyway? How much is there? Does anyone have more hours in a day or minutes in an hour? Within each moment we are alive, don't we have all the time there is, all the time in the world? No wonder the patience of rocks reassures me.

I'm hardly the first to find reassurance in geology. For John Muir, the Scotch-born naturalist whose passionate advocacy for Yosemite helped win it designation as a national park, geologic processes provided a link with the deepest realms of time. "I used to envy the father of our race," he wrote, "dwelling as he did in contact with the new-made fields and plants of Eden; but I do so no more, because I have discovered that I also live in 'creation's dawn.'"

John Muir was arguably the most accomplished apprentice Yosemite has ever nurtured. Early in his first year in California, in 1868, he spent an afternoon in the vicinity of French Bar counting "550 mosses in a quarter of a square inch of a creekside rock." The next summer he signed on to oversee a flock of sheep as they followed the snowmelt, slowly grazing their way from the foothills to the high meadows of the Sierra, and this job gave him endless opportunities to clamber over the mountains, sketching and writing copious notes in the journal he tied to his belt with a thong. He described a Douglas squirrel stripping seeds from the cone of a ponderosa pine and the manic antics of a grasshopper; he classified three types of meadows and their vegetation; he chronicled beetles and butterflies and even bluebottle houseflies. The behavior of everything from ants to bears came under his minute observation.

But the story of the rocks—it both intrigued and eluded him. Once, looking down at the extraordinary features of the Yosemite Valley from his mountain camp, he deemed it "a grand page of mountain manuscript that I would gladly give my life to be able to read. How vast it seems, how short human life when we happen to think of it, and how little we may learn, however hard we try!"

Daunted by the valley, he turned to more accessible mysteries, making note in that same journal entry of giant boulders on the banks of Tamarack Creek:

They mostly occur singly, and are lying on a clean pavement. … They look lonely here, strangers in a strange land. … And with what tool were they quarried and carried? On the pavement we find its marks. The most resisting unweathered portion of the surface is scored and striated in a rigidly parallel way, indicating that the region has been over-swept by a glacier … grinding down the general mass of the mountains, scoring and polishing, producing a strange, raw, wiped appearance, and dropping whatever boulders it chanced to be carrying at the time it was melted.

The entry illustrates a habit that served Muir all his life. Puzzled by the big picture, he turned to direct observation of some individual part—in this case, a few specific boulders—and began with a question: How did they get there? Unable to find evidence that they emerged on the spot, weathered from bedrock, he looked for the agent of their arrival. In retrospect, his observations were not only logical

but also simple; he had only to ask the right questions and keep looking until answers began to reveal themselves. His was a populist science, driven by discipline and passion; it is available to each of us.

Such direct observation spurred Muir on. If he could reason out the history of a few boulders on Tamarack Creek, couldn't the same process lead him to an understanding of Yosemite Valley? In 1871 he quit his job—by then he worked in a sawmill—and devoted himself full-time to scrambling up peaks and down valleys, logging hundreds of miles on foot, studying every creek and basin, every fold and mark on the land that could possibly inform him.

Everywhere he looked, he saw what he took to be the marks of glacial movement, and soon, as a recent biographer, Gretel Ehrlich, phrased it, he was "tracking the footprints of vanished glaciers like a hunter." In October of that year, he found a living glacier on Red Mountain; later that winter he found two more, on Mount Lyell and Mount Maclure. When friends suggested he had discovered only snowbanks, Muir climbed back to elevations over thirteen thousand feet in winter in order to pound in stakes; when he returned a few weeks later the stakes had moved, confirming that "these ice-masses … possess the true glacial motion." He became the first to document live glaciers in the Sierra, and his findings were reprinted in the highly respected *American Journal of Science*.

Though Muir had encountered the study of geology during his two years at the University of Wisconsin a decade earlier, he was not a trained geologist. He trained himself;

in his words, "Patient observation and constant brooding above the rocks, laying upon them for years as the ice did, is the way to arrive at the truths which are graven so lavishly upon them."

His discovery of living glaciers proved that glaciers played a role in Yosemite, but Muir's truths were at odds with other theories about Yosemite's formation current at the time. Josiah D. Whitney, for instance, head of the California State Geological Survey in the 1860s and one of the most respected geologists in the country, denied the importance of glaciers and claimed that Yosemite Valley had been formed during a single cataclysmic event. He deemed the upstart Muir an "ignoramus" and a "mere sheepherder."

In time Muir's theory rose above those of his more educated detractors and became, for nearly a century, the dominant explanation. (Today geologists recognize that glaciers were responsible for the finishing work but not the primary carving.) But to Muir, teasing out the geologic narrative was about much more than being right; it was a matter of spiritual importance. As Frederick Turner explained it:

> What was especially significant for him … was the assumption that the forces that had produced the earth in its present form were still in operation, still acting in the self-same ways they had from the beginning of geological time.
>
> While this … made scientific sense to Muir, it also had a powerful personal appeal for him in that it confirmed the presence of a loving, indwelling divinity. … God had not fashioned this beautiful world in a series of wrathy catastrophes and then gone away

and left it. Instead, He had set in operation forces that had slowly shaped the globe, and in their continued operations one could feel and indeed see the presence of divinity.

Ehrlich called Muir a visionary; Turner deemed him a mystic and hero. He was all these things and more, but first and foremost, he was an observer. The more he looked at nature, the more beauty and order he found in all its aspects, whether brutal or screne. And in this beauty he found evidence of the hand of God. Muir had been raised as a Scottish fundamentalist. Through his study of nature—like the Buddhist-raised Obata and others of many spiritual persuasions who have looked deep enough into the natural world to begin to understand the underlying order on which it operates—he lived in a world in which priests, poets, and scientists shared a common sense of wonder.

Muir disliked the idea of "hiking," which he saw as the dedicated task of getting from one place to another. Like Henry David Thoreau, he preferred to "saunter," perambulating as if he had all the time in the world, stopping to read the clues that natural processes inscribed, counting the minute mosses in a tiny patch of earth or tracing the glacial scars across vast tracts of land.

"As long as I live," he once wrote, "I'll hear waterfalls and birds and winds sing. I'll interpret the rocks, learn the language of flood, storm, and the avalanche. I'll acquaint myself with the glaciers and wild gardens, and get as near the heart of the world as I can."

To get as near the heart of the world as one can—this is what draws us to national parks and wilderness areas. Few will ever attain the genius and dedication John Muir brought to understanding the mountain manuscript. Yet even small kernels of insight reward us.

One afternoon, walking in the meadow below El Capitan, I came upon a small rise. At one time I would have scrambled over it with little notice, perhaps dismissing it as the remnant of a man-made dam. But I had begun to understand the ways of glaciers, and I realized that I stood at a recessional moraine, a spot where fifteen or twenty thousand years ago a glacier had pushed its snout and then retreated, leaving behind a surge in rock and soil like the ridge where a child's finger stops drawing in the sand. Now this remnant spoke to me, a message across the millennia. On top of the moraine I found a fallen log hollowed out by fire and surrounded by sapling ponderosas and realized I had

another dating right at hand ... that the destruction of fire had precipitated the birth of the seedlings.

These are small observations; surely one can live a good life in their absence. And yet the world seems richer by their noting. However challenging or annoying or daunting our own tasks may seem, we are surrounded by rocks and trees, by valleys and rivers shaped by infinitely greater challenges, and still they endure. No matter how starved we feel for time, we suddenly seem to have more of it when we stop long enough to sense the overriding calendar of nature. The chaos that chatters about on the surface of our lives seems to quiet, if only for a moment, and we stand reassured of a deeper consonance.

In 1899 Muir accompanied the E. H. Harriman Alaska Expedition and became particularly fond of Harriman's daughters, Mary and Cornelia, and two of their friends, Elizabeth Averell and Dorothea Draper. The four young women wrote Muir after the trip, and he responded affectionately, closing his letter with advice that summed up the beauty, the pleasure, and the practice of both science and the spirit: "Kill as few of your fellow beings as possible," he advised the girls, "and pursue some branch of natural history at least far enough to see Nature's harmony. Don't forget me. God bless you. Goodbye."

Today Jim Snyder at the Research
Library explained moraines to me
and suggested I climb the hill at the
end of the meadow below El Cap. . . .
I did, and the moraine, the whole
idea of moraine, came into focus.
What I would have scrambled right
over suddenly carried a whole
glacial history with it, and each rock
meant something. Behind a huge
boulder, square as a house, stood the
snag of a burnt tree and a host of
adolescent ponderosas. I realized I
could date the fire by the age of the
new trees. . . .

I've always been fascinated by people who claim
certain habits—a day off, ten hours of sleep a night,
two hours at the gym each day—as necessities,
something nonnegotiable. As a rule, these
people get as much done as anyone else.

I'm beginning to think, more and more, that time is
not real, or at least that it is malleable. Perhaps, like
faith, we have just as much of it as we can handle.
I like the thought of enough time ... that we have
all the time there is, all the time in the world.

I've been reading Muir's <u>My First Summer in the
Sierra</u>, and sometimes he basks in a generosity of
time: "Another glorious Sierra day ... Life seems
neither long nor short, and we take no more heed to
save time or make haste than do the trees and the
stars." But in other moments he yearns for more
time, bemoaning "how short human life when we
happen to think of it, and how little we may
learn, however hard we try!"

Evening Moon
y Chiura Obata

*Apprentice
to Obata*

No one can teach more about reading the great book of nature than John Muir, but he has little to offer when it comes to transferring the sustenance found there to an urban existence. With as much passion as he loved the wild, he hated the metropolis. He became physically ill in cities, and, as the Muir scholar David Robertson has observed, he thought sin and city living were roughly equivalent.

Although Muir's passion sometimes led him to sweeping generalizations, the full breadth of his thinking was more complex. He understood that if we all shared his distaste of urban life and actually abandoned it, the wild he loved would cease to exist. But he can hardly serve as mentor to someone who wants to live more sanely among the complexities of modern city life.

Among those who figure prominently in the history of Yosemite, however, is another model, Chiura Obata, a Japanese artist who arrived in San Francisco as a young man in 1903, when John Muir was sixty-five years old. The two men never met, but they would have liked each other, even as they translated their passion for Yosemite in fundamentally different ways.

I learned of the work of Chiura Obata during my first visit to Yosemite in May 1999. After a hike to Yosemite Falls, my husband and I ended up in the Ansel Adams Gallery. I was looking at maps when Hal came over with a book in his hands. "Look at this," he said. "I think you'll like it."

The book was *Obata's Yosemite: The Art and Letters of Chiura Obata from His Trip to the High Sierra in 1927,* a square book bound in natural linen with a reproduction of Obata's color woodblock print *Evening Moon* on the cover. Even before I opened it, I knew I held something extraordinary in my hands.

The cover image is deceptively simple and in perfect balance: two orange ponderosa trunks stand tall beside a blackened snag, backed by an arc of granite against the lapis lazuli of night. Over it all, a graceful slice of unassuming moon hangs in a sky that grades from darkening night above to the last fade of day at the horizon.

The image possesses a tremendous sense of calm, and it was only later, when I thought about its elements, that I realized the piece isn't simple at all but full of contradictions. Within its juxtaposition of stone and wood, light and dark, life and death, the turning of day into night and back again, it holds the fundamental cycles of our world. That spring, I was looking for calm in the midst of complexity. I still am.

What do we see when we look at a painting? We take in the formal elements: color, composition, form, technique. We respond emotionally to the subject matter or feeling

of the work: whether it strikes us as heavy or light, whimsical or grave, ominous or calm. But a master artist communicates something more through some impalpable mark of commitment: call it wisdom or intention. Obata believed that his biography was written in his paintings. I realize now that *Evening Moon* strikes me not only because it is a singular image but also because it is informed by the very questions I am struggling to understand.

We live our lives by stories. If our brains are computers, as the contemporary metaphor suggests, then stories provide the software, the tools that tell us how to live our lives and expand our sense of what's possible. When I encountered Obata's work that day in the Ansel Adams Gallery, something told me that his story would enlighten me in ways I could hardly yet imagine.

Chiura Obata was born in Sendai, Japan, in 1885 and apprenticed to learn Sumi-e painting when he was seven years old. At fourteen he ran away from home to further his study in Tokyo, two hundred miles south. Tokyo had one of the most dynamic and tumultuous art communities in the world at the time, driven by the clash between the popular embrace of Western painting and a nationalist movement to return to traditional Japanese methods and motifs. Obata became involved with the *nihonga* (Japanese painting) movement that fused both traditions—Western modeling and atmospheric perspective with traditional Japanese aesthetics—and in 1900 he joined the Kensei-Kai, a group of young artists with modern ideas. Three years later, when he set sail for the United States at the age of eighteen, he was already an accomplished artist.

Japonisme, Japanese style, was the rage in America, and stories about the success of Japanese artists who ventured there circulated around Tokyo. If such possibilities drove Obata, he was quickly disappointed. Interest lay in Japanese tradition rather than in the innovative work that Obata was exploring, and whatever popularity Japanese arts enjoyed, Asians themselves faced brutal discrimination. Spat on and bullied in the streets, Obata was once arrested during a street brawl but released when the police realized that eight men had attacked him.

But Obata found ways to employ his talents, supporting himself as an illustrator for Japanese-language publications and winning occasional commissions to design department store windows and stage sets. When the 1906 earthquake brought the walls of his apartment house down around him, he found himself a refugee in a public park. At that point he did what came most naturally: he started to sketch. He was the first and possibly the only artist to gain permission to enter the heart of the earthquake zones and record what he saw. Perhaps it was during that chapter of his life, when the activity of recording the disrupted world around him saved him from despair, that he realized that art was not only his calling and support but a way to live fully in even the most trying circumstances.

By 1920 Obata was well established in the Japanese art community and had made inroads into the broader California art scene. From his youthful training in Tokyo, he knew that East and West had much to offer each other aesthetically; in San Francisco, he came to believe that the cross-pollination of artistic traditions could overcome discrimination as well. In 1921 he helped bring together a group of American, Japanese, Chinese, and Russian artists to form the East West Art Society. There he met Perham Nahl, who later became head of the Art Department at the University of California, Berkeley; in 1932 Nahl asked Obata to join him there. Obata's classes in Sumi-e ranked among the most popular in the department, and his students remember him as full of energy, passion, and humor as well as an unshakable calm.

Calm: the word attaches to Obata throughout his long life, regardless of how demanding the external factors were. As war rhetoric heated up in Japan, anger and racism against Asians grew more virulent over here. Obata was juggling the demands of his young family, his students, and his professional friendships and commitments. His wife, Haruko, managed their home and helped him in the studio, but she had her own life as an artist as well, teaching and demonstrating *ikebana,* the Japanese traditional art of flower arranging, of which she was a master.

Calm was a matter of discipline for Obata, something he practiced through attention to nature, realized through his art, and passed on through his teaching. As one of his students, "Skinner" (Millicent Ward Niesen), recalled, his teaching began with instruction

in how to use materials, grinding the ink slowly while focusing on the blank paper and imagining the painting to come. Obata insisted his students work from direct observation, and they often painted outside. Sometimes he took them to the mountains or along the shore; other days they went no farther than the campus gardens. Years later, Niesen remembered the impact of that training: "How little, in our daily lives, do we really, truly look at things around us, particularly nature? Mr. Obata taught us to observe, observe, observe. … We had, perhaps, never felt so close to nature. In later years, when the young were beginning to awaken to the importance of the natural world in their lives, we had only to … relive our time with Mr. Obata to understand."

Such experience did not, of course, turn what Niesen described as "brash, impatient Western students" into Zen monks; Obata knew the value of melding traditions rather than replacing one with another. As Niesen explained, "Wise Perham Nahl had not introduced … Mr. Obata to turn us all into imperfect practitioners of Japanese art, but to introduce us to a philosophy and discipline which would stay with us all our lives."

Obata first visited Yosemite in 1927 on a six-week camping trip with his friend Worth Ryder, a painter who had recently joined the arts faculty at Berkeley. Both men were avid hikers, but they didn't plan to rough it: they set out in a car loaded with "two beds, fourteen boxes of food, painting materials, fishing gear, two suitcases, a tent, a large saw, a large axe, a big shovel, and a big bucket of water in case of emergency," as Obata wrote in his first letter home to his wife, Haruko. "Most people smile at us, thinking we are going to the mountains to find gold." Two weeks later the sculptor Robert Howard joined them.

Yosemite intrigued Obata immediately. He vowed to paint a hundred paintings during his time there and wasted no time getting started: on the first day he began sketching in the car as Ryder drove. They set up camp near Buck Meadows and began a ritual that continued after Howard joined them and through several base camps: rising early and setting off on vigorous hikes; intense days of painting; late afternoons of fishing; and long evenings of cooking, conversation, and sake around the campfire. Ryder made a great stew; Obata became famous for his sukiyaki with dried tofu and the sweet grass he had gathered during the day; sometimes the tall old Irish park ranger, Tim Sullivan, would stop by with his mules, White and Blue, and grill up some steaks. Howard later recalled their nights around the campfire with particular affection: "After [dinner], before turning in for sleep, Obata would bring forth his philosophies of life, how to remain young, how to appreciate every minute of existence and time, how right it was to be happy and cheerful and productive, how wrong to shed tears, do nothing and waste time and strength. That to be an artist was best of all things."

Obata wrote home with pleasure about how strong he was becoming, and how browned by the sun, but it was as an artist that Yosemite excited him most. Non-Native artists had been intrigued with the grandeur of the Yosemite Valley since they first arrived with explorers in the mid-1800s. Painters such as Thomas Hill and Keith Clark gained national attention for their sweeping views, and when Alfred Bierstadt painted Yosemite, he exaggerated the height of its peaks and the unearthly quality of its light in order to create religious allegories infused with both transcendent grace and patriotic rigor, something subsequent generations of painters sentimentalized to the point of tiresome cliché. By the turn of the century, serious artists deemed Yosemite unpaintable.

Obata saw it anew, on a closer, more intimate scale. "It would surely take three or four years to sketch only the meadow flowers," he wrote to Haruko. He preferred the high country, likening the bumper-to-bumper traffic in the valley to "a school of sardines," but

even there, in the midsummer crush, he found calm in the midst of chaos, and his paintings of Yosemite Valley landmarks have a quiet, unromanticized beauty.

Yosemite marked a coming of age for Obata as a painter; he had his first major one-man exhibition a year after his initial trip. Although he selected pieces from among the more than ten thousand paintings he had created since his arrival in America twenty-five years earlier, the body of the show came from his work in the High Sierra.

After his first trip in 1927, Obata returned to Yosemite nearly every summer, bringing with him his family and friends and sometimes teaching there as well. Over the years, his classes at Berkeley grew increasingly popular and influential; he and Haruko ran a successful studio in Berkeley, and their son and daughter-in-law opened a second branch in Oakland; and Obata showed his work in prestigious galleries and museums in California and across the country.

Then, with the Japanese bombing of Pearl Harbor on December 7, 1941, everything changed. Within four months, Obata and his family were interned in a horse stall at Tanforan Racetrack outside San Francisco, sleeping on mattresses they had stuffed with hay themselves; a few months later they were evacuated to the middle of a windy desert in west Utah, at Topaz Relocation Camp.

When Robert Howard wrote affectionately about Obata's tendency to wax philosophic around the campfire, he added that Obata's enthusiasms were not "idle talk. … Obata lives his beliefs and more. He influences those who know him to live deeply and well." Howard's intuition about Obata in that halcyon summer of 1927 proved particularly true through the dark years of World War II.

As soon as it became clear that the Japanese community would be relocated, officials at UC Berkeley tried to find refuge for the Obatas. Monroe Deutsch, vice-president and provost, asked the National Park Service to allow the family to reside at Yosemite. This request was forwarded to the Fourth Army at the Presidio in San Francisco, and on April 2, Assistant Adjutant General Hugh T. Fullerton replied with a classic catch-22: "No reason is apparent as to why Japanese Americans should not be permitted to reside in Yosemite National Park … [but] Proclamation no. 4 has been issued which prevents Japanese residents of Military Area No. 1 from crossing the eastern boundaries thereof." In other words, the Obatas could live in Yosemite, but they couldn't enter it to do so. On April 30, they and the rest of the Berkeley Japanese community were consigned to Tanforan.

Even before Deutsch's request for refuge was denied, Chiura had decided he would stay with his community. He, Haruko, and the rest of the family had been packing and disposing of their belongings for weeks. From the beginning Obata acted without bitterness. A week before the evacuation, he sold over a hundred paintings and designated the proceeds to fund a scholarship "for the student, regardless of race or creed, who … has suffered the most from this war."

Obata started recording the internment from the moment he set foot in the First Congregational Church, the staging area from which internees were transported to Tanforan. As he sketched a small child playing peek-a-boo with a soldier, he had a revelation: "Seeing that scene in a situation where we were being forced into an unreasonable evacuation, to kill the burning heart, burning determination of these young people was very bad." He resolved to start an art school to "maintain one spot of normalcy." Three days after he arrived at Tanforan, he submitted a plan for the school; it opened less than a month later, with sixteen instructors offering twenty-three courses in everything from figure painting to fashion design. Soon Haruko joined the faculty and added *ikebana* to the curriculum. Ninety classes a week attracted over six hundred students, elementary school age through adult. Exhibitions of student work traveled to Mills College, UC Berkeley, and the Berkeley YWCA; shows within the compound drew enthusiastic attendance and greatly improved morale.

When the Tanforan internees were moved to the Central Utah Relocation Center in the Utah desert, Obata immediately reorganized the school there. It was so popular that a second branch soon formed on the far side of the camp.

If accommodations at Tanforan had seemed austere, at least the climate was familiar; the Utah camp, named Topaz after Topaz Mountain visible in the distance, was inconceivably remote, in the middle of a vast, bleak desert that suffered from blistering heat in the summer and subzero cold in the winter. Dust storms often darkened the sky. "Even indoors we wore scarves and masks because the dust was like a fog in the room," Haruko recalled, adding that she swept the floor so often that Chiura called her a "human vacuum cleaner."

Obata's memories of Yosemite sustained him during these difficult times. Koho Yamamoto, now a prominent Sumi-e artist in New York, was a teen when she started studying with Obata at Topaz, and she remembers that her *sensei* (teacher) often talked about his beloved Sierra and painted favorite Yosemite scenes from memory. But in time he came to find a beauty in the starkness of Topaz, in the changing light at sunrise and sunset, and in the complex mix of color throughout the day. "I feel profound gratitude for these things," he wrote years later, "and in that sense, to put it briefly, I did not feel abandoned. Instead, I learned a lot. If I hadn't gone to that kind of place I wouldn't have realized the beauty that exists in that enormous bleakness."

Obata believed that appreciation of beauty, achievable through artistic practice, would help his community not only survive but thrive. His hopes were realized as many at both Tanforan and Topaz had experiences similar to the student who wrote that evacuation had left him in a state of despair until "by recommendation of a friend I began to study painting under Obata *sensei*. ... I began to feel that I had found a place of calm. ... This is due to Sensei's charm that comes from the spirit of brush painting and his enthusiastic teaching. I made up my mind that whatever will happen in the future and however hard I have to work, I will never lose this spirit of painting."

By the time the Obatas were released from Topaz in the spring of 1943, Chiura had created over two hundred paintings and drawings that chronicled every aspect of the Japanese internment experience. He had also touched the lives of literally hundreds of students.

In 1945, with the lifting of the exclusion order, the Obatas returned to California, and Chiura resumed his position at UC Berkeley as well as his frequent visits to Yosemite. He retired from Berkeley in 1954, the same year he became an American citizen (people of Japanese birth were not allowed to apply for American citizenship until 1952), and began leading tours to Japan, further promoting mutual understanding between his two beloved cultures. In his final years, when he had grown too infirm to travel, he continued to return to Yosemite through the power of memory, as he had during his years of internment, painting favorite scenes of the Sierra in the quiet shade of his garden. He died in 1975 at the age of ninety.

On my second visit to Yosemite, in the fall of 2000, I determined to experience the park under Obata's guidance, and I tucked *Obata's Yosemite* into my backpack, along with a bottle of sake. My friends Dorothee and Diana and I made base camp at May Lake, and on the day we climbed Mount Hoffman we returned to enjoy Dorothee's eggplant Punjab, a good portion of the sake, and the glorious range of conversation that high mountain air, comfortable fatigue, good food, and the balm of friendship inspire. It was late when we retired, yet I wasn't ready for sleep. I read *Obata's Yosemite* by headlamp and then got up to walk around. I made my way down to the lake, leaned back against a rock still warm from the day's sun, and looked up at an indigo sky hung with a sliver of moon—Obata's moon.

In the great peace I enjoyed at that moment, the frantic scurry of my city life seemed far away, but I couldn't help thinking how my trivial concerns paled in comparison to the experiences that Obata and his family had endured. Now that I have spent more time under his tutelage, I expect he would have told me that such comparisons are useless.

His first visits to Yosemite had been as charmed and uncomplicated as my own, and he wrote home with the same pleasure in the high mountain air and in the beauty of the rocks and the streams that I felt that night by May Lake. "I only feel full of gratitude," he told Haruko. "I want to bring you and our friends here, and I will." Years later, in the midst of vastly changed circumstances, a similar gratitude infused him as he came to appreciate the beauty of the bleak desert at Topaz, and once again he acted to share that appreciation with others. What Obata stressed to his students, and what the example of his life offers us now, is the importance of paying attention to Great Nature, as he called it, wherever we find it and trusting that such attention will sustain us through good and ill.

"Nature gives us endless rhythm and harmony in any circumstance," he told a group of women artists in San Francisco during the heart of the Great Depression, "not only when we are on a joyous path, but even in the depth of despair. … If we keep appreciation in the depth of our hearts … our feeling will become as clear as full moonlight."

Today I have been consciously trying to paint like Obata, not because, in the end, I want to paint in his manner, for his style is uniquely his own, but because it makes me pay closer attention to what intrigues me in his work. Even in this, he instructs me. Obata studied in Japan under Gaho Hashimoto, who urged him to "copy everything good" but to "imitate no one."

I am loving this trip of discovery and realizing that yet another apprenticeship I am serving is how to be a painter, how to work fully and well in such a place.
I think of Robert Howard's description of Obata: "Every pause for rest saw Chiura at work. This is almost the first impression he gives one, either working or on his way to work; never getting ready. Just somehow always ready, for at least a brief sketch."

Afterword

It is mid-June in Salt Lake City, and I'm hot on the trail of a mystery. I've been trying to find pockets of the wild in this metropolis, and yesterday I visited Hidden Hollow, a small natural area along Parley's Creek in the neighborhood known as Sugar House. Although the hollow's few hundred yards of trail are next to a mall and within a stone's throw of the interstate, it provides a surprising oasis of calm, buffered from the sounds of the freeway by a thick canopy of maples, cottonwoods, and willows.

When I arrived, the late-afternoon sun filtered through the trees and lit the stream, which glowed red as if infused with strawberry juice. I'd never seen such a color before and drew closer to find a weedy mass of red plants wafting in the slow-moving water all along the south bank.

I squatted down and pulled out a small tuft of red woody fibers that looked almost like root hairs except that they didn't seem attached to anything bigger; they grew right out of the muddy streambed. I couldn't identify them, so I took my sample to the Utah Museum of Natural History. There, Ann Kelsey, the head of collections, put it under the microscope, and we tried to key it out but failed—what we imagined might be leaves branching off the main stems followed no regular pattern; when we cut into them, the bodies we thought might be flowers held only woody material. Ann suggested my sample simply had to be roots, so I am back today digging in the mud, trying to figure out what they attach to, floundering once again without success. In the meantime, Ann is showing the sample to other botanists at the museum, and I have sent out queries to an informal network of local naturalists. Within the next few days, someone will come up with an answer. For now, I'm simply tickled to find this puzzling blush of growth in a creek next to a shopping center.

I have been trying to look at my urban environment with some of the attention and curiosity that come so naturally when I am in a place like Yosemite. I have tracked a vole in the snow near the condominium in which my husband and I spent the winter and watched a water ouzel blink the river from its eyes on a rock in the middle of City Creek. I find such surprises all around me as if they have magically appeared at my request. "Seeing is believing," the old saw goes, but it takes only an act of attention to realize that sometimes we have to believe before we can see.

With this attention comes a new connection to this city, even a sense of ownership. I will come back from time to time to check on the red growth in Parley's Creek and watch how it changes with the seasons. I have a stake in this length of stream now; it has become part of my home ground. The pleasure of this intimacy reminds me of something Bill Rutherford, Salt Lake's urban forester, told me recently: one reason he likes his job so much is that he gets to know and look after individual trees in a way that was impossible when he worked in the national forests.

"So does this mean that you won't go back to Yosemite or other places like it?" my friend Dorothee asked me recently as we walked in the foothills above Salt Lake. The answer is no. Whenever I have the opportunity to go deep into the backcountry of Yosemite or another wilderness, I will take it. But perhaps if I incorporate the wild that survives even in this metropolis into my daily life, I won't need to "escape" quite so often or depend so much on frequent short trips that often lead me to the very places most impacted by visitors.

When Wallace Stegner wrote that we need wilderness to save us from our termite lives, he addressed a split between the urban world and the natural one that many of us now take for granted. But however much wilderness and other open spaces restore us, they can survive only if we don't ask too much of them.

"Life is so short, we must move very slowly," holds an old Thai proverb. Perhaps it follows that the wild is so rare, we must find it everywhere.

My mystery is solved. The raspberry-colored
roots belong to the big peachleaf willow trees
that line the bank. The thick mat that
wafts in the stream is a weave of root hairs
finer than eyelashes that branch off of only
slightly thicker threads that in turn branch off
of string-like roots and so on, gaining thickness
and strength until they reach back all the way to
the huge twisty roots that break out of the
ground near the base of the trees and support
them to their sixty- and seventy-foot heights.
I knew that willow roots hold stream banks
together, but this is the first time I've had a
real sense of their density and complexity.

The blanket of roots in the water teases
apart into delicate threads.

The leaves are five or six inches long and look like those on peach trees, hence the name, peachleaf willow (<u>Salix amygdaloides</u>).

Straight and shiny on the tree, they begin to wither and curl almost the moment a branch hits the ground.

Acknowledgments

Thanks to the many friends who have accompanied me to Yosemite at various times: my dear husband, Hal Cannon; Dorothee Kochs and Diana Sterne; Larry Kirkland and Brendan Doyle. I am especially grateful to Dorothee for her conversations and insights throughout the preparation of this book.

Thanks, too, to the new friends and colleagues who have taught me so much about Yosemite's natural and human history: Tom Bopp, the pianist at the Wawona Hotel, and his wife, artist Diane Detrick Bopp; the naturalist Michael Elsohn Ross; Jim Snyder and Linda Eade at the Yosemite Research Library; and Rangers Shelton Johnson and C. Ferguson. Bill Rutherford, Ann Kelsey, Sylvia Torti, and Ty Harrison helped me transfer some of the knowledge I was gleaning in Yosemite to my hometown.

Janice T. Driesbach and Susan Landauer introduced me to Chiura Obata through their excellent book *Obata's Yosemite,* which led me in turn to *Topaz Moon: Chiura Obata's Art of the Internment* by Kimi Kodani Hill. My own book would have been impossible without these previous works. In addition, Hill is Obata's granddaughter and the family archivist, and she generously answered tons of questions, led me to other sources, and granted permission for the reproduction of Obata's *Evening Moon.* I am grateful, too, to Obata's students, Koho Yamamoto and Millicent Ward "Skinner" Niesen, for their recollections.

Sources

Browning, Peter, ed. *John Muir in His Own Words: A Book of Quotations.* Lafayette, CA: Great West Books, 1988.

Cushman, John H., Jr. "Priorities in the National Parks." *New York Times,* July 26, 1998.

Dean, Dennis R. "Muir and Geology." *John Muir: Life and Work,* ed. Sally M. Miller. Albuquerque: University of New Mexico Press, 1993, pp. 168–193.

Driesbach, Janice T., and Susan Landauer, eds. *Obata's Yosemite: The Art and Letters of Chiura Obata from His Trip to the High Sierra in 1927 with Essays by Janice T. Driesbach and Susan Landauer.* Yosemite National Park, CA: Yosemite Association, 1993.

Ehrlich, Gretel. *John Muir: Nature's Visionary.* Washington, DC: National Geographic Society, 2000.

Fullerton, Hugh T. Letter to John B. Wosky, Acting Superintendent, Yosemite National Park, April 2, 1942. Yosemite National Park Archives.

Gifford, Terry, ed. *John Muir: His Life and Letters and Other Writings.* Seattle: The Mountaineers, 1996.

Harvey, H. T., H. S. Shellhammer, R. E. Stecker, and R. J. Hartesveldt. *Giant Sequoias.* Three Rivers, CA: Sequoia Natural History Association, Inc., 1981.

Hill, Kimi Kodani. *Topaz Moon: Chiura Obata's Art of the Internment.* Berkeley, CA: Heyday Books, 2000.

Howard, Robert. "Obata Gets Spirit of California." *Obata's Yosemite,* eds. Janice T. Driesbach and Susan Landauer. Yosemite National Park, CA: Yosemite Association, 1993.

Huber, N. King. "A History of the El Capitan Moraine." *Yosemite* 64, 1 (James B. Snyder): 2–6.

———. *The Geologic Story of Yosemite National Park.* Yosemite National Park, CA: Yosemite Association, 1989.

Kodani, Mrs. Eugene. Letter to Jack Gyer, National Park Service, December 6, 1975. Yosemite National Park Archives.

Miller, Sally M., ed. *John Muir: Life and Work.* Albuquerque: University of New Mexico Press, 1993.

Muir, John. *My First Summer in the Sierra.* San Francisco: Sierra Club Books, 1988.

Niesen, Millicent Ward ("Skinner"). "A Few Memories of Mr. Chiura Obata." Unpublished, Kimi Kodani Hill personal archives, 1996.

O'Neill, Elizabeth Stone. *Mountain Sage: The Life Story of Carl Sharsmith, Yosemite Ranger/Naturalist.* Groveland, CA: Albicaulis Press, 1996.

Peattie, Donald Culross. *A Natural History of Western Trees.* Boston: Houghton Mifflin Company, 1953, 1991.

Robertson, David. *West of Eden: A History of the Art and Literature of Yosemite.* Yosemite National Park, CA: Yosemite Natural History Association and Wilderness Press, 1984.

Ross, Michael Elsohn. *Nature Art with Chiura Obata.* Naturalist's Apprentice Series. Minneapolis, MN: Carolrhoda Books, 2000.

Schaffer, Jeffrey P. *Yosemite National Park: A Natural-History Guide to Yosemite and Its Trails,* 4th ed. Berkeley, CA: Wilderness Press, 1999.

Stegner, Wallace, and Wayne Owens. *Wilderness at the Edge.* Layton, UT: Gibbs Smith Publisher, 1991.

Stoll, Mark. "God and John Muir." *John Muir: Life and Work,* ed. Sally M. Miller. Albuquerque: University of New Mexico Press, 1993, pp. 64–81.

Turner, Frederick. *Rediscovering America: John Muir in His Time and Ours.* New York: Viking, 1985.

Vale, Thomas R., and Geraldine R. Vale. *Walking with Muir Across Yosemite.* Madison: University of Wisconsin Press, 1998.

Wolfe, Linnie Marsh. *John of the Mountains: The Unpublished Journals of John Muir.* Boston: Houghton Mifflin Company, 1938.

Yamamoto, Koho, interviewed at the Koho School of Sumi-e in New York City, February 21, 2002.

Zwinger, Ann. *Yosemite: Valley of Thunder.* The Genesis Series. San Francisco: Tehabi Books, HarperSanFrancisco, 1996.

About the Author

Teresa Jordan is the award-winning author of *Riding the White Horse Home: A Western Family Album*, *Field Notes from the Grand Canyon*, *Cowgirls: Women of the American West*, and she has edited two collections of women's writing. The recipient of the Western Heritage Award from the Cowboy Hall of Fame for scriptwriting and literary fellowship from the National Endowment of the Arts as well as many other literary awards, she lives in Salt Lake City with her husband, public radio producer Hal Cannon. *Field Notes from Yosemite* is the second book in her series of Sketchbook Expeditions.